To Simon and Lilie

First published in 2025 in France as Beaucoup, Beaucoup d'Animaux.
This 2026 edition first published in North America by Boxer Books.

ISBN 978-1-4547-9899-6

Boxer Books titles may be purchased in bulk for business, educational, or promotional use.
For more information, please contact your local bookseller or the Hachette Book Group's Special Markets department at special.markets@hbgusa.com.

Printed in China

Lot #: 10 9 8 7 6 5 4 3 2 1
01/26

Translation by Christele Jolys
Extra animal facts by Harriet Blackford
Fact checked by Matthew Rendle, RVN Veterinary Nurse, chair of the Association of Zoo & Exotic Veterinary Nurses (AZEVN).

Illustration note: animal pictures are not to scale and are not representative of the actual scale of one animal to another.

LOTS AND LOTS OF ANIMALS

According to scientists, there are more than 10 million animal species living on Earth, of which only about 2 million are known and classified.

This classification evolved over the centuries and is now based on the relationships between living and extinct species. It classifies living beings based on the characteristics they share (vertebrae, feathers, beak, etc.) and which are inherited from a common ancestor.

Here is an illustrated inventory of 2,500 land and sea animals from around the world, some known and others lesser-known . . .

Marlène Normand

BOXER BOOKS

INSECTS

Insecta

common mosquito
Asian tiger mosquito
blue hoplia
bee beetle
horned corydalid
common antlion
European honeybee
yellow-legged termite
German cockroach
common bombardier beetle
oriental hornet
Asian hornet
earwig
buff-tailed bumblebee
large bee-fly
orchid mantis
two-colored mason bee
European hornet
snow flea
beautiful demoiselle
Madagascar hissing cockroach
violet carpenter bee
thorny devil mantis
scorpionfly
striped bug
emerald cockroach wasp
common wasp
Colorado potato beetle
common mantis
green shield bug
firebug
European rhinoceros beetle
giant leaf insect
Southern green shield bug
heath click beetle
bluebottle fly
red longhorn beetle
emperor dragonfly
fifteen-spotted ladybug
steelblue ladybug
cherry fruit fly
comma ladybug
seven-spotted ladybug
red froghopper
giant Malaysian stick insect
fourteen-spotted ladybug
Chinese grasshopper
false Colorado potato beetle
eyed ladybug
twenty-two-spotted ladybug
mountain cicada

BUTTERFLIES AND MOTHS

Lepidoptera

dimorphic ermine moth
ornate tiger moth
monarch
scalloped oak
common buckeye
Northern chequered skipper
pine processionary moth
Madagascar comet moth
long-tailed skipper
Danubian march moth
Diana fritillary
luna moth
bumblebee hawk-moth
magpie moth
eight-spotted forester moth
bilberry emerald
mint moth
pine crambus moth
great mormon
common copper
hawthorn white butterfly
oak hairstreak
reseda white butterfly
Queen Alexandra's birdwing
silver-washed fritillary
dragon-tailed butterfly
orange tip
cabbage moth
chimney sweeper moth
hornet moth
Ionian emperor butterfly
large chequered skipper
blue frosted banner
banded king shoemaker
lesser swallow prominent
green oak tortrix
leopard lacewing
common bluebottle
coltsfoot plume moth
large white
boxwood moth
antimachus
lappet
apple clearwing moth
hedge beauty
red cracker butterfly
scarce crimson and gold
swallowtail
five-bar swordtail
blue morpho
new Caledonian blue butterfly
fruit-tree tortrix moth
forester
Alpine tiger moth
batis noctuid moth

SPIDERS, SCORPIONS, AND HORSESHOE CRABS

Chelicerata

common house spider
silver argiope
cucumber green spider
wasp spider
green lynx spider
green huntsman spider
red-backed jumping spider
Chinese golden scorpion
purseweb spider
harvestman
false black widow
fencepost jumping spider
yellow fat-tailed scorpion
cardinal spider
deathstalker scorpion
tree orb-weaver
strawberry spider
African fat-tailed scorpion
sombre wolf spider
Bolivian dwarf tarantula
golden silk orb-weaver
coneweb spider
pumpkin patch tarantula
European garden spider
black fat-tailed scorpion
Corsican trapdoor spider
running crab spider
pirate wolf spider
emperor scorpion
giant forest scorpion
cat-faced Spider
Indian red scorpion
Middle East fat-tailed scorpion
common yellow scorpion
huntsman spider
sand running crab spider
Asian forest scorpion
Sisyphus' cobweb spider
woodlouse spider
pine theridion
Antilles pinktoe tarantula
Mexican redknee tarantula
green crab spider
Atlantic horseshoe crab
David Bowie's golden spider

CRUSTACEANS

Crustacea

spotted reef crab
batwing coral crab
common prawn
African giant shrimp
common shrimp
velvet crab
Antarctic krill
edible crab
Indian white prawn
giant freshwater prawn
tiger pistol shrimp
caramote prawn
coral crab
sea star shrimp
amethyst shrimp
Sally Lightfoot crab
giant tiger prawn
Norway lobster
European spiny lobster
cardinal shrimp
Florida stone crab
royal spiny lobster
pea crab
pink spiny lobster
crinoid shrimp
elegant hermit crab
European spider crab
circular crab
blue shrimp
elegant squat lobster
golden crab
Kuruma prawn
Prideaux's hermit crab
yeti crab
mitten crab
scarlet shrimp
common hermit crab
harlequin shrimp
Mexican dwarf crayfish
white-spotted hermit crab
spiny squat lobster
coconut crab
shame-faced crab
stone crab
Caribbean spiny lobster
Smith's mantis shrimp
banded cleaner shrimp

TURTLES, TORTOISES, TERRAPINS

Testudines

spiny turtle
Malayan box turtle
Matamata turtle
Indian star tortoise
spiny softshell turtle
yellow-spotted Amazon river turtle
Arrau river turtle
leopard tortoise
parrot-beaked tortoise
box turtle
Asian leaf turtle
Northern map turtle
olive ridley sea turtle
geometric tortoise
painted turtle
African helmeted turtle
softshell turtle
alligator snapping turtle
marginated tortoise
pig-nosed turtle
spotted turtle
common snapping turtle
Hermann's tortoise
pancake tortoise
loggerhead sea turtle
Aldabra giant tortoise

CROCODILES, ALLIGATORS, CAIMANS

Crocodilia

Chinese alligator
mugger
crocodile
Orinoco crocodile
Philippine crocodile
Schneider's
smooth-fronted
caiman
dwarf crocodile
black caiman
yacare caiman
African slender-snouted
crocodile
Siamese
crocodile
American
crocodile
freshwater
crocodile
American
alligator

SERPENTS AND SNAKES

Serpentes

ornate flying snake
black mamba
green jararaca
Madagascan tree boa
rainbow snake
gaboon viper
scarlet kingsnake
Saharan horned viper
tentacled snake
green python
Madagascar leaf-nosed snake
Montpellier snake
Indian cobra
carpet python
red-headed coral snake
green grass snake
Forsskal's snake
red-tailed pipe snake
Mexican burrowing snake
Lataste's viper
common death adder
Arabian sand boa
rough-scaled bush viper
Malabar pit viper
royal python
asp viper
Jamaican boa
braid snake
green anaconda

LIZARDS, CHAMELEONS, IGUANAS, VARANS

Lacertilia

Madagascar day gecko
spiny-tailed monitor
brown anole
pinocchio lizard
Jackson's chameleon
ocellated lizard
central bearded dragon
Madagascar girdled lizard
many-colored bush anole
Texas horned lizard
crocodile monitor
Asian water monitor
Pyrenean rock lizard
Catalan wall lizard
horned tree lizard
frilled lizard
zebra-tailed lizard
Mexican beaded lizard
common agama
frog-eyed gecko
moorish gecko
spotted flying dragon
gila monster
Burton's legless lizard
emerald tree monitor
Eastern bearded dragon
armadillo lizard
giant girdled lizard
common barking gecko
leopard gecko
giant ameiva
Timor monitor
thorny devil
curly-tailed lizard
emerald swift
sand lizard
common basilisk
Argentine black and white tegu
common side-blotched lizard
slow worm
Manapany day gecko
knight anole
banded arboreal alligator lizard
common wall lizard
common tegu
Northern alligator lizard
European glass lizard
blue-tailed day gecko
desert iguana
Spencer's monitor
red-eyed crocodile skink
warty chameleon

FROGS, TOADS, NEWTS

Amphibia

annam toad
Great Plains toad
dyeing poison dart frog
Asian horned frog
Western spadefoot
hellbender
Kihansi spray toad
Seychelles frog
long-toed salamander
Italian cave salamander
four-toed salamander
Plains spadefoot toad
Texas blind salamander
red salamander
long-tailed salamander
yellow-bellied toad
blue-spotted salamander
Northern two-lined salamander
oriental fire-bellied toad
Northern dusky salamander
Mandarin newt
olm
Brazilian horned frog
Northwestern salamander
spotted toad
common mudpuppy
Argentine horned frog
red-backed salamander
Western red-backed salamander
Western spadefoot toad
Ambrosi's cave salamander
common toad
Japanese fire-bellied newt
spotted salamander
Malagasy rainbow frog
Indian bullfrog
spiny toad
American toad
Solomon Island horned frog
Fiji ground frog
lovely poison frog
Lycian salamander
Alpine salamander
Anderson's crocodile newt
Eastern tiger salamander
African common toad
pickerel frog
golden poison frog
Wallace's flying frog
boreal chorus frog
Vietnamese mossy frog
California red-legged frog
edible frog

SNAILS, SLUGS, SEA SLUGS, OYSTERS

Gastropoda and Bivalvia

black slug
cellar slug
tapestry turban
zebra snail
common cockle
leopard slug
Desmoulin's whorl snail
garden slug
geography cone
red slug
Roman snail
Venetian snail
common door snail
seminole ramshorn
Pyrenean snail
Pacific banana slug
girdled snail
bat volute
shameless nudibranch
garden snail
marbled aplexa
gray field slug
giant doris
pink phyllidia
white-lipped snail
yellow-dotted purple doris
four-lined nudibranch
large gray snail
Dalmation doris
striped tritonia
glossodoris pallida
Corsican snail
faithful seaslug
Willan's chromodoris
crested aeolis
Bohol discodoris
great scallop
Kunie's chromodoris
African doris
Hypselodoris orsinii

OCTOPUSES AND SQUIDS
Cephalapoda
glacial squid
Humboldt squid
blue-ringed octopus
giant Pacific octopus
colossal squid
whip-lash squid
common octopus
Dana octopus squid
musky octopus
curled octopus
shortfin squid
Atlantic white-spotted octopus
bigfin squid
Caribbean reef octopus
dumbo octopus
mimic octopus
wonderpus octopus
greater argonaut

ram's horn squid
California two-spot octopus
Saluzzi's octopus
day octopus
North Atlantic octopus
Caribbean reef squid
chambered nautilus
miter squid
veined octopus
bigfin reef squid
Atlantic brief squid
veined squid
broadclub cuttlefish
European common squid
pharaoh cuttlefish
striped pyjama squid
paintpot cuttlefish
European squid
flamboyant cuttlefish
Atlantic bobtail squid
bobtail squid
red flying squid
Japanese flying squid
giant cuttlefish
Joubin's squid
purpleback flying squid
umbrella squid
hydrothermal vent octopus
vampire squid
common cuttlefish
giant squid

JELLYFISH, SEA URCHINS, STARFISH

Cnidaria

variable fire urchin
Rousseau sea urchin
purple sea urchin
radiant sea urchin
burrowing urchin
long-spined sea urchin
banded sea urchin
crowned sea urchin
Atolla jellyfish
violet sea urchin
upside-down jellyfish
compass jellyfish
crowned jellyfish
warty sea star
flower urchin
blue blubber jellyfish
long-armed starfish
lagoon jellyfish
sun star
red starfish
common brittle star
contractile sea cucumber
horned sea star
barrel jellyfish
Hefferman's starfish
black brittle star
royal starfish
seven-armed sea star
black jellyfish
Indian sea star
red-knobbed starfish
common starfish
mauve stinger
biscuit star
knobbly starfish
red cushion starfish
red mesh starfish
pencil urchin
sea pig
red lance urchin
melon sea urchin
black sea urchin
common feather star
the red comatulid
elephant ear anemone
pillar coral
whisker coral
green star polyp coral
elkhorn coral

FISH
Actinopterygii
blue tang
dwarf lionfish
European smelt
golden perch
guinea fowl puffer
Atlantic bluefin tuna
red handfish
grayling
red phantom tetra
Peter's elephantnose fish
golden trevally
ram cichlid
rummy-nose tetra
cardinal tetra
freckled hawkfish
goliath grouper
orbicular batfish
red-bellied piranha
Asian arowana
spotted scat
flag-tailed fish
spotted boxfish
Nile tilapia
neon tetra
electric eel
ocean sunfish
kissing gourami
Japanese pufferfish
goldspotted eel
foxface rabbitfish
black bullhead catfish
Alaska pollock
longhorn cowfish
whiting
paradise fish
goldfish
guppy
lined surgeonfish
Atlantic cod
silver moonyfish
devil scorpionfish
Mediterranean moray
beluga
European sturgeon
European eel
twinspot lionfish
snowflake moray
opah
Moorish idol
convict surgeonfish
fire goby
longnose hawkfish
dorado
Atlantic mackerel
American paddlefish
unicorn fish
dwarf hawkfish
pumpkinseed
pilot fish
spotted drum
haddock
Northern pike
blobfish
striated frogfish
Indo-Pacific sailfish
coalfish
Siamese fighting fish
common remora
common carp
long snouted lancetfish
common barbel
Indian glassy fish
goliath tigerfish
black ruby barb
European plaice
arapaima

European seabass
Red Sea raccoon butterflyfish
four-eyed butterflyfish
emperor angelfish
blue-girdled angelfish
flame angelfish
axilspot hogfish
blackspot seabream
mandarinfish
garfish
ornate wrasse
African butterflyfish
kaluga sturgeon
barred thicklip wrasse
kribensis
green severum cichlid
pinecone fish
princess of Burundi
long-spined porcupinefish
Atlantic herring
humphead wrasse
European anchovy
Pastel ringwrasse
European pilchard
blue discus
pearlscale cichlid
orange-lined triggerfish
queen triggerfish
European bullhead
threespot dascyllus
scissortail sergeant
clown triggerfish
Midas cichlid
flying gurnard
ribbon eel
Talbot's demoiselle
common clownfish
Amazon leaffish
frontosa cichlid
swallowtail sea perch
oscar fish
comber
royal gramma
golden damselfish
European perch
freshwater angelfish
golden rainbow trout
venustus hap
blue parrotfish
slender grouper
bicolor parrotfish
barreleye fish
giant squirrelfish
longnose gar
red lionfish
Atlantic salmon
yellow-banded sweetlips
pygmy seahorse
comet or marine betta
common dab
reef stonefish
humpback grouper
oarfish
spotfin lionfish
turbot
spotted seahorse
Atlantic wolffish
Atlantic flyingfish
European hake
alligator gar
black seadevil
anglerfish
short-snouted seahorse
swordfish
leafy seadragon
sea goldie
purple queen anthias
brown trout
great barracuda

RAYS AND CHIMAERAS

Batoidea and Holocephali

panther
electric ray
straightnose
rabbitfish
mangrove
whipray
common
eagle ray
giant
eagle ray
spiny
butterfly ray
elephant fish
Brazilian
electric ray
giant
electric ray
ornate
eagle ray
ocellate river stingray
Round
Fantail Ray
bluespotted
ribbontail ray
pelagic stingray
green sawfish
reef
manta ray
small-eyed ray
mirror
ray
white skate
porcupine ray
common torpedo
spotted
eagle ray
common skate
common sawfish
reticulate
whipray
cuckoo ray

SHARKS

Selachii

bigeye sand tiger shark
winghead shark
blacknose
shark
bull shark
Mexican hornshark
spiny
dogfish
zebra
shark
whale shark
coral
catshark
starspotted
smooth-hound
nursehound
whitetip
reef shark
shortfin mako shark
Ganges
shark
tiger shark
pelagic
thresher
gray
reef shark
goblin shark
smooth
hammerhead shark
starry
smooth-hound
small-spotted
catshark
saddle carpetshark
great hammerhead
swell
shark
Galapagos
catshark
salmon shark
porbeagle
nurse shark

WHALES, KILLER WHALES, DOLPHINS, NARWHALS

Cetaceans

gray whale
Atlantic
humpback dolphin
Northern
bottlenose whale
Blainville's
beaked whale
North Atlantic
right whale
harbor
porpoise
hourglass
dolphin
bottlenose
dolphin
sperm whale
narluga
Amazon
river dolphin
Cuvier's
beaked whale
pantropical spotted dolphin
minke whale
false killer whale
tucuxi
Atlantic
white-sided dolphin

SEA LIONS, SEALS, MANATEES

Sirenians and Pinnipeds

Australian sea lion
Subantarctic fur seal
sea lion pup
crabeater seal
harp seal
Steller sea lion
leopard seal
gray seal
fur seal
California sea lion
ribbon seal
South African fur seal
New Zealand sea lion
Caribbean manatee
Antarctic fur seal

PRIMATES
Primates
cotton-top tamarin
celebes crested macaque
sunda slow loris
coquerel's sifaka
gray mouse lemur
gee's golden langur
golden-mantled tamarin
mantled guereza
pygmy marmoset
ring-tailed lemur
silvery marmoset
emperor tamarin
Western red colobus
red-shanked douc
Bornean orangutan
Philippine tarsier
sooty mangabey
indri
aye-aye
pileated gibbon
moustached guenon
Talapoin monkey
Western gorilla
common marmoset
black lemur
greater spot-nosed monkey
black bearded saki
bonnet macaque
agile gibbon
common chimpanzee
yellow baboon
black spider monkey
lion-tailed macaque

common
woolly monkey
Sumatran
orangutan
mandrill
black-faced
lion tamarin
golden
snub-nosed
monkey
gelada
Nepal gray langur
Prince
Bernhard's titi
bonobo
Tonkin snub-nosed
monkey
woolly spider
monkey
patas monkey
dusky leaf
monkey
Eastern
gorilla
Senegal
bushbaby
Bengal
slow loris
crowned
lemur
grivet
proboscis
monkey
golden lion
tamarin
monk saki
siamang
black-and-
white ruffed
lemur
Northern night monkey
pied tamarin
bald uakari
common
brown lemur
hamadryas
baboon
Tapanuli
orangutan
red-handed howler

WOLVES AND FOXES
Canidae
raccoon dog
swift fox
maned wolf
dingo
pale fox
side-striped jackal
Ethiopian wolf
wolf pup
short-eared dog
Arctic fox
tundra wolf
Great Plains wolf
Arctic wolf
common gray wolf
South American gray fox

black-backed jackal
domestic dog
coyote
fennec fox
Rüppell's sand fox
puppy
hoary fox
red fox
kit
Tibetan fox
dhole
bat-eared fox
gray fox
African wild dog
bush dog
Mexican wolf
kit fox
Arabian wolf
corsac fox
golden jackal
cape fox
Darwin's fox
crab-eating fox

LIONS, TIGERS, LEOPARDS, CATS

Felidae

ocelot
serval
snow leopard
Southern tiger cat
cheetah
jaguarundi
rusty-spotted cat
cougar
caracal
kodkod
Andean
mountain cat
flat-headed
cat
clouded
leopard
bay cat
wildcat
tiger
leopard cat

HYENAS, GENETS, MONGOOSES
Feliformia
three-striped palm civet
masked palm civet
golden palm civet
fossa
rusty-spotted genet
Indian gray mongoose
Indian brown mongoose
white-tailed mongoose
black mongoose
Egyptian mongoose
banded linsang
Malagasy civet
Cape genet
giant forest genet
spotted hyena
ring-tailed mongoose
Owston's palm civet
meerkat
dwarf mongoose
Malayan civet
aardwolf
Javan mongoose
marsh mongoose
yellow mongoose

Asian palm civet
crested genet
Grandidier's mongoose
large-spotted civet
Abyssinian genet
African civet
brown hyena
Angolan genet
Somalian slender mongoose
spotted linsang
Liberian mongoose
otter civet
banded mongoose
common genet
Cape gray mongoose
large Indian civet
binturong
black-footed mongoose
narrow-striped mongoose
Hose's palm civet
small Indian civet
brown-tailed mongoose
easter falanouc
striped hyena
banded palm civet
slender mongoose
bushy-tailed mongoose

HORSES AND ZEBRAS

Equidae

kiang
domestic donkey
African wild ass
donkey
foal
onager
Przewalski's horse

BULLS, BISONS, BUFFALOES

Bovidae

yak
bongo
bushbuck
common eland
calf
lowland
anoa
lesser kudu
kouprey
domestic water buffalo
zebu
buffalo calf
African buffalo

SHEEP, CHAMOIS, GOATS

Caprinae

Rocky Mountain goat
urial
Sumatran serow
long-tailed goral
Formosan serow
markhor
Japanese serow
Alpine ibex
Himalayan tahr
musk ox
kid

WILD BOARS, PIGS, HIPPOPOTAMUSES

Suina and Hippopotamidae

Bornean bearded pig
Palawan bearded pig
desert warthog
common warthog
black Limousin pig
Basque black pig
Western white pig
Bayeux pig
hippopotamus
pygmy hippopotamus
large white pig
Sulawesi warty pig
Gascon pig
piglets

MICE, SQUIRRELS, RABBITS, HARES

Rodents and Lagomorphs

West Siberian lemming

cactus mouse

Eastern chipmunk

red squirrel

short-tailed chinchilla

Utah prairie dog

pygmy flying squirrel

Mexican red-bellied squirrel

North American porcupine

pacarana

Barbary ground squirrel

Guinea pig

woodland jumping mouse

Plain's pocket gopher

white-faced spiny tree-rat

Pel's flying squirrel

meadow jumping mouse

Brazilian porcupine

Central American agouti

striped ground squirrel

Asiatic brush-tailed porcupine

springhare

lowland paca

European rabbit

nutria

Siberian chipmunk

cream-colored giant squirrel

red-crested tree rat

Black rat

volcano rabbit

Patagonian mara

Eurasian beaver

Indian crested porcupine

California mouse

wood mouse

Arctic hare

red-tailed squirrel

African brush-tailed porcupine

ricefield rat

Siberian flying squirrel

Botta's pocket gopher

Alpine marmot

ondatra zibethicus

Eastern gray squirrel

Indian giant squirrel

tree porcupine

Gunnison's prairie dog
Sumatran striped rabbit
red pika
lesser Egyptian jerboa
desert gundi
Northern pika
desert cottontail
common gundi
the forest giant squirrel
tuco-tuco
greater cane rat
gray-collared chipmunk
Northern pocket gopher
ashy-colored chinchilla rat
North American beaver
pygmy rabbit
collared pika
crested porcupine
red-rumped agouti
Eastern cottontail
rock Rat
European hare
black-tailed prairie dog
common acouchi
American pika
mountain beaver
Amami rabbit
marsh rabbit
Malayan porcupine
camas pocket gopher
plains viscacha
Afghan pika
naked mole-rat
Malabar spiny dormouse
degu
mountain viscacha
common vole
capybara
Mechow's mole-rat
Chacoan mara
lesser jerboa
California pocket mouse
Northern birch mouse
Riverine rabbit
desert kangaroo rat
long-eared jerboa
silky pocket mouse
European hamster
golden hamster
Russian dwarf hamster
forest dormouse
garden dormouse
edible dormouse
woodland dormouse
hazel dormouse

HEDGEHOGS, MOLES, SHREWS
Eulipotyphla, Afrosoricida, and Dermoptera
lowland streaked tenrec
Etruscan shrew
Eastern European hedgehog
Asian house shrew
masked shrew
crowned shrew
Daurian hedgehog
Russian desman
elegant water shrew
Crawford's gray shrew
Northern short-tailed shrew
star-nosed mole
North African sengi
ornate shrew
hairy-tailed mole
web-footed tenrec
Brandt's hedgehog
Bendire's shrew
European hedgehog
common shrew
lesser white-toothed shrew
greater white-toothed shrew
Pyrenean desman
tailless tenrec
bicolored shrew
long-eared hedgehog
Arctic shrew
Eurasian water shrew
Townsend's mole
Javan short-tailed gymnure
Southern African hedgehog
Bornean smooth-tailed treeshrew
American shrew mole
Indian hedgehog
Grant's golden mole

long-tailed mole
checkered elephant shrew
black and rufous elephant shrew
four-toed hedgehog
moonrat
Sunda flying lemur
pen-tailed treeshrew
Indian treeshrew
four-toed elephant shrew
lesser hedgehog tenrec
North American least shrew
forest shrew
Somali hedgehog
desert hedgehog
gray-faced sengi
Algerian hedgehog
greater hedgehog tenrec
Nimba otter shrew
large-eared tenrec
Asian mole shrew
broad-footed mole
giant otter shrew
Somali elephant shrew
Northern white-breasted hedgehog
elephant Shrew
European mole
Hispaniolan solenodon
Caucasian mole
taiga shrew
pygmy shrew
Cape golden mole
common treeshrew

WEASELS, OTTERS, SKUNKS

Mustelidae, Mephitidae, and Procyonidae

Saharan
striped polecat
American
hog-nosed skunk
Southern
spotted skunk
striped skunk
striped
hog-nosed skunk
crab-eating
raccoon
American
badger
Guadeloupe
raccoon
Japanese
marten
hooded
skunk
yellow-throated
marten
Molina's
hog-nosed skunk
greater
hog badger
wolverine
Chinese
ferret-badger
European mink
Asian badger
Sunda stink
badger
Cozumel
Raccoon

BEARS AND PANDAS

Ursidae and Ailuridae

red panda
grizzly bear
bear cubs
polar bear
sloth bear
American
black bear

DEER, ROE DEER, ELK

Cervidae

little red brocket
red brocket deer
Bornean yellow muntjac
marsh deer
fawn
elk
pampas deer
barasingha
Persian fallow deer
red deer
Indian muntjac
Indian hog deer
mule deer
Northern pudu
chital deer
Calamian deer

GAZELLES, WILDEBEEST, ANTELOPES
Bovidae
Cuvier's gazelle
dama gazelle
black-fronted duiker
bohor reedbuck
waterbuck
red-fronted gazelle
sable antelope
yellow-backed duiker
Bates's pygmy antelope
hirola
Arabian oryx
black wildebeest
addax
common duiker
mountain gazelle
saiga antelope
black duiker

Salt's dik-dik
mountain reedbuck
Günther's dik-dik
Swayne's hartebeest
springbok
blesbok
oribi
Kirk's dik-dik
East African oryx
blue wildebeest
zebra duiker
Zanzibar suni
blackbuck
impala
gerenuk
royal antelope
gray rhebok
steenbok
beira antelope
puku

GIRAFFES, LLAMAS, DROMEDARIES, CAMELS

Giraffidae and Camelidae

Bactrian camel
South African
giraffe
alpaca
West African
giraffe
Masai giraffe
okapi
guanaco

RHINOCEROSES, ELEPHANTS, TAPIRS, HYRAXES

Proboscidea, Perrisodactyla, and Hyracoidea

white rhinoceros
Southern
tree hyrax
rhino calf
black rhinoceros
Brazilian tapir
Sumatran
rhinoceros
Javan rhinoceros
Indian rhinoceros
Asian elephant
mountain tapir
Baird's tapir

ARMADILLOS AND SLOTHS

Xenarthra, Tubulidentata, Pholidota, and Monotremes

pygmy three-toed sloth
pale-throated sloth
Indian pangolin
Sunda pangolin
tree pangolin
giant pangolin
Southern tamandua
seven-banded armadillo
Philippine pangolin
dwarf armadillo
hairy long-nosed armadillo
giant anteater
aardvark
Brazilian three-banded armadillo
Southern long-nosed armadillo

KANGAROOS AND OPOSSUMS
Marsupials
mouse opossum
crest-tailed mulgara
elegant fat-tailed mouse opossum
gray short-tailed opossum
long-nosed bandicoot
lemur-like ringtail possum
Eastern pygmy possum
striped possum
Goodfellow's tree-kangaroo
Western barred bandicoot
red kangaroo
dusky pademelon
feathertail glider
Doria's tree-kangaroo
Eastern quoll
black-striped wallaby
common brushtail possum
common wombat
numbat
black tree-kangaroo
Southern hairy-nosed wombat
parma wallaby
Sulawesi bear cuscus
Eastern gray kangaroo
antilopine kangaroo
yellow-footed rock-wallaby
Southern marsupial mole
kowari
monjon
dingiso

water opossum
long-nosed potoroo
common spotted cuscus
Western gray kangaroo
Lumholtz's tree-kangaroo
brown-eared woolly opossum
red-necked pademelon
silky shrew opossum
quokka
greater glider
Virginia opossum
spectacled hare-wallaby
red-necked wallaby
Northern common cuscus
rock-wallaby
white-eared opossum
common ringtail possum
common opossum
Matschie's Tree-kangaroo
short-eared rock-wallaby
Scott's tree-kangaroo
Eastern bettong
Clara's echymipera
Eastern barred bandicoot
gray-bellied dunnart
rufous rat-kangaroo
wallaroo
banded hare-wallaby
grizzled tree-kangaroo
Tasmanian devil
squirrel glider
Southern brown bandicoot
monito del monte
feather-tailed possum
slender-tailed dunnart
honey possum
rufous hare-wallaby
agile wallaby
greater bilby
koala

BATS
Chiroptera
Eastern red bat
Honduran white bat
Egyptian fruit bat
greater bulldog bat
hammer-headed bat
Seychelles fruit bat
Northern ghost bat
greater sac-winged bat
horseshoe bat
Blasius's horseshce bat
spectacled flying fox
common noctule
spotted bat
painted bat
European free-tailed bat
hoary bat
straw-colored fruit bat
Indian flying fox
common pipistrelle
brown long-eared bat

greater ghost bat
yellow-winged bat
giant dog-faced bat
Western barbastelle
greater noctule bat
golden-capped fruit bat
greater horseshoe bat
Spix's disk-winged bat
greater false vampire bat
Queensland tube-nosed bat
Antillean ghost-faced bat
Azores noctule
gray-headed flying fox
Australian ghost bat
lesser mouse-tailed bat
Wagner's mustached bat
common vampire bat
greater mouse-eared bat
Malayan flying fox
black flying fox

BIRDS

Aves

laughing falcon
peregrine falcon
greater roadrunner
coral-billed ground-cuckoo
channel-billed cuckoo
African pygmy falcon
guira cuckoo
harpy eagle
Egyptian vulture
barn owl
bald eagle
European nightjar
red-headed vulture
Great Nicobar serpent eagle
tawny fish owl
common nighthawk
common kestrel
powerful owl
Oilbird
scale-feathered malkoha
Sumatran ground cuckoo
giant coua
golden eagle

Andean condor
Eurasian pygmy owl
Sunda frogmouth
pearl Kite
lesser sooty owl
Northern white-faced owl
secretarybird
king vulture
spectacled owl
tawny frogmouth
barred forest falcon
red kite
saker falcon
Montagu's harrier
Eurasian eagle-owl
brahminy kite
tawny owl
Eurasian sparrowhawk
Eurasian scops owl
chestnut-bellied cuckoo
little cuckoo
turkey vulture
crested caracara
common cuckoo
red-legged seriema
great potoo
black caracara
oriental bay owl
snail kite
black-faced coucal

capuchinbird
Malayan banded pitta
bare-necked umbrella bird
Eurasian wren
long-tailed manakin
golden-headed manakin
white-cheeked starling
spotted forktail
Sri Lanka hill myna
great tit
pied monarch
brown shrike
common blackbird
pompadour cotinga
Guianan cock-of-the-rock
blue cotinga
forest fody
Southern red bishop
russet sparrow
twelve-wired bird-of-paradise
Wilson's bird-of-paradise
king bird-of-paradise
blue bird-of-paradise
long-tailed finch
rufous-breasted bush robin
garden warbler
azure-winged magpie
Eurasian magpie
superb starling
psarocolius viridis
house sparrow
lesser bird-of-paradise
yellow-billed oxpecker
flame bowerbird
European robin
blue-gray gnatcatcher
varied tit
common chaffinch
common raven
South Island saddleback
tūī
crested treeswift
glossy swiftlet
common hill myna
yellow-backed oriole
red-headed weaver
pied crow
blue jay
carrion crow
red bird-of-paradise
chucao tapaculo
white-throated needletail
scarlet finch
passerina amoena
yellow-crowned gonolek
telophorus dohertyi
bluethroat
Western jackdaw
black-and-red broadbill
common house martin
hemiprocne comata
green cochoa
Japanese grosbeak
helmet vanga
barn swallow
superb lyrebird
green lora
regent bowerbird
mesitornis variegatus
great bustard
rufous-tailed rock thrush
purple martin
Asian fairy-bluebird
short-toed treecreeper
mountain owlet-nightjar
Eastern golden weaver
regal sunbird
Western bluebird
black bustard
chestnut weaver
red-cheeked cordon-bleu
red-whiskered bulbul
fire-tailed sunbird
whinchat
ruby-throated hummingbird
Eurasian jay
short-tailed green magpie
blue-faced honeyeater
blue-banded pitta

African blue flycatcher
white-headed munia
Northern mockingbird
common myna
Java sparrow
Javan leafbird
amethyst starling
diamond firetail
gouldian finch
ruby-topaz hummingbird
silver-breasted broadbill
cinnamon hummingbird
red-winged fairywren
black-throated bushtit
mallee emu-wren
yellow-bellied sunbird-asity
dusky lark
cinnamon becard
royal flycatcher
black-tailed tityra
ocellated tapaculo
cedar waxwing
yellow-cheeked becard
varzea schiffornis
ufous-capped antthrush
black-cheeked gnateater
green broadbill
black phoebe
long-tailed broadbill
jambu fruit dove
pink-headed fruit dove
hooded pitta
Northern black korhaan
blue-winged pitta
rock wren
New Zealand pigeon
many-colored fruit dove
Torresian imperial pigeon
Costa's hummingbird
pompadour green pigeon
European turtle dove
white-eared brown dove
masked dove
black-and-yellow broadbill
Anna's hummingbird
topknot pigeon
wire-crested thorntail
orange fruit dove
cloven-feathered dove
spotted dove
broad-billed hummingbird
violet-tailed sylph
scaly-naped pigeon
thick-billed green pigeon
purple-tailed imperial pigeon
wonga pigeon
great cuckoo-dove
scaled pigeon
West Peruvian dove
Western crowned pigeon
white-collared swift
superb fruit dove
white-faced cuckoo-dove
pheasant pigeon
spinifex pigeon
brush bronzewing
common wood pigeon
elegant imperial pigeon
tambourine dove
crested pigeon
rock dove
tooth-billed pigeon
blue-headed quail-dove
Pacific emerald dove
diamond dove
speckled wood pigeon
coleto
Seychelles blue pigeon
blue ground dove
laughing dove
ruddy cuckoo-dove
Victoria crowned pigeon
white-breasted ground dove
Nicobar pigeon
cinnamon ground dove
pink-necked green pigeon
black-faced sandgrouse

European roller
yellow-billed kingfisher
great jacamar
black bee-eater
green-tailed jacamar
Northern flicker
violet turaco
black-headed parrot
Eurasian wryneck
red-breasted parakeet
rainbow bee-eater
blue-and-yellow macaw
great tinamou
small-billed tinamou
emu
forest kingfisher
speckled mousebird
dusky lory
crimson rosella
common kingfisher
quebracho crested tinamou
European green woodpecker
rufous-necked puffbird
great spotted woodpecker
emerald toucanet
citron-throated toucan
spot-billed toucanet
greater flamingo
Australian king-parrot
Northern carmine bee-eater
hoatzin
toucan barbet
pale-mandibled aracari
Lord Derby's parakeet
Sumatra trogon
gray-breasted mountain toucan
common ostrich
Southern brown kiwi
toco toucan
fire-tufted barbet
cockatiel

scarlet macaw
pitta-like ground roller
pale-headed rosella
maroon shining parrot
rosy-faced lovebird
European bee-eater
green wood hoopoe
long-tailed ground roller
resplendent quetzal
Pesquet's parrot
blue-bellied roller
Eurasian hoopoe
military macaw
orange-breasted trogon
Guinea turaco
rufous-necked hornbill
ed-headed trogon
white-crested turaco
rufous motmot
red-billed hornbill
great hornbill
great blue turaco
white-crowned hornbill
bearded barbet
palm cockatoo
Andean motmot
Andean flamingo
black-breasted puffbird
greater rhea
Southern cassowary
black-backed dwarf kingfisher
Cuban tody
sun parakeet
golden parakeet
cuckoo roller
Abyssinian ground hornbill
red-and-yellow barbet
red-headed barbet

great black-backed gull
Cape petrel
Southern royal albatross
gray crowned crane
white stork
corn crake
wattled jacana
marabou stork
Persian shearwater
Western grebe
saddle-billed stork
Dalmatian pelican
hooded grebe
painted stork
black-headed gull
great cormorant
little auk
little pengui
scarlet ibis
gray-backed storm petrel
snow petrel
Northern bald Ibis
crested Ibis
Southern rockhopper penguin
Atlantic puffin
erect-crested penguin
white-faced storm petrel
magnificent frigatebird
Adélie penguin
black stork
tufted puffin
great blue heron
jabiru
yellow-crowned night heron
Northern fulmar

Arctic tern
demoiselle crane
Sabine's gull
Eurasian spoonbill
great crested grebe
Pacific loon
shoebill
sacred ibis
gray heron
semipalmated sandpiper
crested auklet
razorbill
squacco heron
Australasian darter
king penguin
emperor penguin
sarus crane
African penguin
gentoo penguin
kagu
common guillemot
Chinese pond heron
ibisbill
brown booby
water rail
agami heron
imperial shag
blue-footed booby
royal spoonbill
anhinga
great white pelican
little egret
red-billed tropicbird
sunbittern
Australasian gannet

Muscovy duck
ringed teal
mountain quail
domestic chicken
Bulwer's pheasant
Canada goose
green junglefowl
mallard
common shelduck
snow goose
mute swan
cygnets
knob-billed duck
red-breasted goose
Australian shelduck
blue-billed curassow
bufflehead
Palawan peacock-pheasant
white-faced whistling du
greater sage-grouse
kelp goose
Western capercaillie
king eider
gray partridge
blue peafowl
common quail
redhead duck

painted spurfowl
surf scoter
red-crested pochard
California quail
spot-winged wood quail
red junglefowl
white eared pheasant
rufous-throated partridge
wild turkey
see-see partridge
green pheasant
ocellated turkey
chicks
Sri Lanka junglefowl
buff-throated partridge
rock ptarmigan
crested partridge
Elliot's pheasant
fulvous whistling duck
king quail
blood pheasant
maleo
golden pheasant
Australian brush-turkey
rock partridge
orange-footed scrubfowl
Temminck's tragopan
malleefowl
Himalayan monal
vulturine guinea fowl
koklass pheasant
harlequin duck
ruffed grouse
Cabot's tragopan
crested guinea fowl
Moluccan scrubfowl
Northern screamer
black-fronted piping guan
hooded merganser
graylag goose
mandarin duck

LOTS AND LOTS OF ANIMALS

Take a closer look at the animal families that appear in this book. What do they have in common? What makes them different? Do the families have any special features? Discover fascinating answers to these questions and lots and lots of fabulous facts!

INSECTS INSECTA pages 6–7

Insects are the most successful group of animals on Earth. More than one million species have been discovered so far! They belong to the big group of animals called arthropods. This is the largest group in the animal kingdom.

Insects are invertebrates, which means they do not have a backbone. In fact, they don't have any bones at all and their outside is hard. It's called an exoskeleton. Their body is divided into three parts; a head with antennae and mouthparts, a thorax with six legs and usually wings, and an abdomen.

Some insects have hearing organs on their legs, they breathe through the sides of their bodies, and they are able to smell from either their mouth or antennae!

Insects are vital for life on our planet. They pollinate flowers, they get rid of plant and animal remains by eating them, and they are a huge source of food for other animals. Birds are estimated to eat 400–500 tons a year!

BUTTERFLIES AND MOTHS LEPIDOPTERA pages 8–9

Butterflies and moths are insects. They start life as larvae, called caterpillars, and spend all their time eating and growing until they form a case called a pupa. Inside this case, they undergo a complete transformation—and burst out as a butterfly or moth. This is called metamorphosis.

Butterflies generally fly during the day and have antennae with an obvious club end whereas moths generally fly at night and have various types of antennae. However, there are exceptions—some moths fly during the day, and some butterflies are active in the evening.

Most butterflies and moths feed on nectar. Their mouthparts look like a long tube called a proboscis, that they can push into flowers to get at the nectar.

There are some really big species of butterflies such as the Queen Alexandra's birdwing with a wingspan up to 12 inches. And some really tiny species such as Stigmella maya with a wingspan of ⅛ of an inch.

SPIDERS, SCORPIONS, HORSESHOE CRABS CHELICERATA pages 10–11

These animals are grouped together because their mouthparts, called chelicerae, are clawlike or fang-like. They are arthropods, just like insects, but they have two parts to their body instead of three—a head and an abdomen.

Spiders have fangs that can inject venom to immobilize their prey. Some also spin webs to trap their prey in the sticky silk. Ticks and mites have fangs that act more like scissors so they can cut into flesh to allow them to drink the blood.

Scorpion fangs are small and near their mouths. They are used to tear up their prey and pass it into their mouths. The large pincerlike claws you can see are called pedipalps and are used for protection and killing prey. They also have a sting in their tail!

Horseshoe crabs do not look like spiders or scorpions, but they do have chelicerae mouthparts which are used to chop up their food and pass it into their mouths.

CRUSTACEANS CRUSTACEA pages 12–13

Crustacean means crusty one! These animals are arthropods, too. They mainly live in water. Some, such as woodlice, live on land in damp areas, like under logs. The biggest crustacean is the Japanese Spider Crab with a leg span of 12.5 feet. The smallest is a tiny parasite only measuring 0.1 millimeters.

Like all arthropods, crustaceans must shed their hard outsides to grow bigger. They are vulnerable during this time until their skin hardens. Although there is a crab, called the hermit crab, that uses empty shells to live in. Once it has outgrown its shell, it looks for a bigger empty shell, then scuttles across to slip inside before it is caught by a hungry predator.

Crustaceans are an important food source for humans. We eat shrimp, prawns, lobsters, and crabs, and harvest over seven million tons a year.

Krill is the name given to small shrimplike crustaceans that are extremely important in the seas and oceans. They are a major food source for many animals including the biggest animal in the world, the blue whale.

TURTLES, TORTOISES, TERRAPINS TESTUDINES pages 14–15

Turtles, tortoises, and terrapins belong to the group of animals known as reptiles. Reptiles are vertebrates which means they have a backbone. They have scaly skin and are "cold blooded." This means their bodies cannot automatically keep their blood at the same temperature all the time. That's why reptiles love to bask in the sun! The most obvious thing about these reptiles is the hard shell covering their bodies. This is made mainly from their rib bones.

Turtles live in the sea and come out on to beaches to lay their eggs. When the eggs hatch, the babies have to make a dash to the sea to avoid being eaten by seagulls and other predators.

Tortoises live on land and can tuck their heads and legs into their shells for protection. The giant tortoise found on the Galapagos Islands can live to more than 100 years.

Terrapins spend their time between ponds and waterholes and the land. Some can live in brackish coastal areas as well. Although they have their own name, "terrapin," they are really just small turtles.

CROCODILES, ALLIGATORS, CAIMANS CROCODILIA pages 16–17

These animals are reptiles. They like to spend their time in rivers and lakes. Alligators stay mainly in freshwater whereas crocodiles can live in seawater.

Crocodilians are very good swimmers and use their muscular tails to drive them forward through the water. Their skin is very thick and covered in scales. They are carnivores, which means they eat meat, and have lots of teeth to hang on to their prey which they swallow without chewing.

Crocodiles lay their eggs on land in a nest and the mother looks after the young once they hatch. This is unusual in reptiles, who mostly fend for themselves.

Crocodilians used to share the earth with dinosaurs and are thought to be the closest living relative to birds.

SERPENTS AND SNAKES SERPENTES pages 18–19

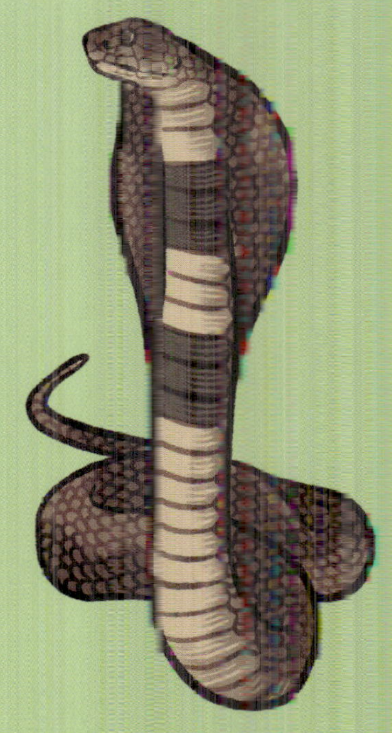

Snakes are reptiles with no legs. They have scaly elongated bodies with long, thin organs to fit inside.

Most snakes are predators. Some have venom they inject with their special front teeth to paralyze their prey. Others, known as constrictors, squeeze their prey to death with their strong, muscular bodies.

Snakes swallow their prey whole. They have special jaws that can open very wide to allow them to swallow prey much larger than their mouths.

Snakes have no eyelids so they cannot close their eyes. Their tongue is forked and flicks in and out of their mouths. It is used to "sniff" the air and the ground to find their prey.

Most snakes lay eggs but there are some, for example, the boa constrictor, that grow their babies in their bodies and give birth.

LIZARDS, CHAMELEONS, IGUANAS, VARANS

LACERTILIA pages 20–21

Lacertilian reptiles are lizards and lizard-like reptiles, such as iguanas, geckos, skinks, and so on. They have enormous variety of form with neck frills, spines, and spikes. Some can detach their tails when threatened to allow them to escape predators. Eventually, their tails will regrow.

There are a few lizards that have lost their limbs through evolution, such as the slow worm, and so they look like snakes but are actually legless lizards.

The largest lizard is the Komodo dragon at nearly 10 feet long. It can kill a water buffalo. It has venom glands in its mouth which stops blood clotting.

Chameleons can change their color to help them blend into their background and they have eyes that can swivel independently. Their tongues are twice as long as their bodies and they flick it out to catch food. The males also change color to impress the females.

Some lizards can run up walls and across ceilings due to their specialized feet.

FROGS, TOADS, NEWTS AMPHIBIA pages 22–23

Amphibians are vertebrates and, like reptiles, they are cold blooded. They are not scaly but have smooth, often moist, skins, through which they breathe.

Frogs have strong back legs and jump well. Toads have warty skin and hop rather than jump. They both have sticky tongues that dart out of their mouths to catch their food, such as flies.

Amphibians live mainly in or near fresh water although they have adapted over time to live in many different habitats. For example, the female red-eyed tree frog in the Amazon lays her eggs on a leaf that overhangs a pond. When the tadpoles hatch, they fall into the water to continue their development.

Most amphibians lay their eggs in water and the baby frogs or toads (tadpoles) that hatch out look nothing like the adults. They change through a process called metamorphosis into the adult form gradually, growing their legs and losing their gills and eventually emerging from the pond as mini adults.

Salamanders look more like lizards in shape. Most are small but the Chinese giant salamander can grow to 6.5 feet. Their young called larvae have gills and teeth and some species can keep their "baby" traits into adulthood, like the axolotl.

SNAILS, SLUGS, SEA SLUGS, OYSTERS

GASTROPODA AND BIVALVIA pages 24–25

These animals are mollusks. Mollusks are invertebrates and are a very diverse group of animals which includes slugs, octopuses, mussels, and clams.

Gastropods have a muscular foot used for movement and a rasp-like "tongue" with tiny teeth for scraping up food.

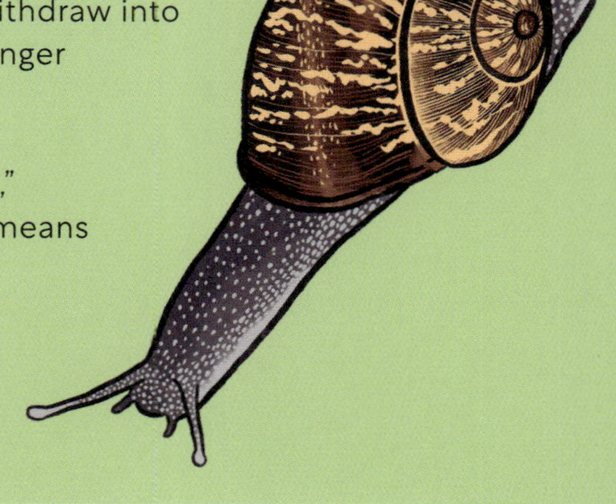

Gastropods are found in water and on land. Snails have a coiled shell. Those that live on land can withdraw into their shells for protection. Their shells help to keep their bodies moist. Slugs and nudibranchs no longer have shells or only have a small vestige of a shell. They have found other ways to remain moist.

Nudibranchs are very beautiful and have been given descriptive names such as "sea rabbit," "dragon," and "marigold." They store stinging cells in their bodies taken from the prey they have eaten which means they can sting.

Slug bodies are mostly water and to keep themselves moist they make a lot of mucus. They eat plant matter and can cause a lot of damage in gardens and farmers' fields.

OCTOPUSES AND SQUIDS CEPHALAPODA pages 26–27

Cephalopods are mollusks and live in the seas and oceans. They have very little shell, which is inside their bodies. They have tentacles and big eyes.

The giant squid is the largest living invertebrate at a length of more than 65 feet, including its extended tentacles. The smallest is a tiny squid at approximately ¾ of an inch.

Cephalopods are unique among invertebrates in that they are considered to have a brain of sorts. Studies have shown that the octopus can learn and has intelligence. Tool-using has been seen in the veined octopus which takes coconut shells from the seabed and carries them to use as portable shelters.

Most cephalopods have color pigment cells and can change their color for camouflage and to communicate with others. They can also produce ink when threatened as this hides their escape route.

Cephalopods can use jet propulsion to move by squirting water out of their body.

JELLYFISH, SEA URCHINS, STARFISH CNIDARIA pages 28–29

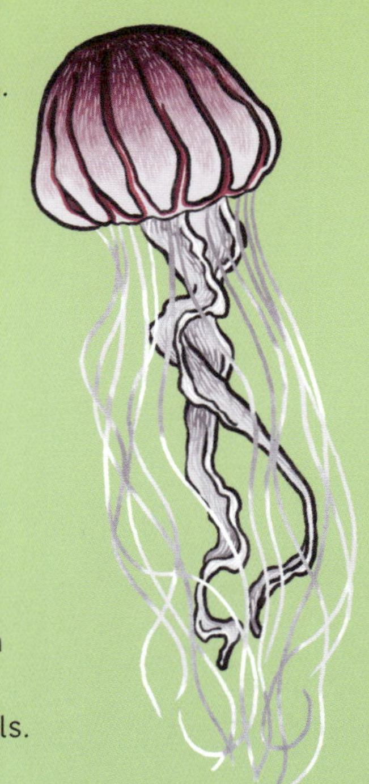

Cnidarians and echinoderms are invertebrates and live in freshwater and the sea. Cnidarians include corals, jellyfish, and sea anemones. These animals have jellylike, bell-shaped bodies with tentacles and stinging cells. The tentacles surround the mouth, which is the only opening to the body, so it is also the exit for waste. The stinging cells in the tentacles are used to capture prey. Corals are tiny cnidarians that live in colonies and create enormous coral reefs that are an important habitat in the sea for many other animals.

Echinoderms have a central disc with five or more arms surrounding it. They have tubelike feet that they move around on by means of a hydraulic system.

Starfish are predators, hunting other marine invertebrates. Some species can push their stomachs out of their mouths to digest prey bigger than themselves. Brittle stars use their long, thin arms to crawl across the sea floor.

Most sea urchins are round spiky balls but there are some that have a flatter shape to burrow easily into the sandy seabed. Their bodies are made up of five parts arranged around a central point, like the segments of an orange. They move around on their tube feet, but they can also propel themselves using their spines. Some have venom in their spines. Sea urchins are mainly vegetarian, eating algae, but they will also eat some animals.

FISH ACTINOPTERYGII pages 30–31

Fish are vertebrates. They live in water and use gills to get oxygen from the water. Their bodies are covered in scales and they have fins for swimming. Although fish are cold-blooded, bigger and very active fish, such as tuna and the white shark, can hold a higher temperature in their core compared with the water temperature. These fish have a swim bladder that is filled with gas and allows the fish to stay at depth in the water.

There is a huge variety in shape and style of fins, as well as in their color and number. Some fish, like the electric eel, can generate an electric field and give anything nearby a shock. Seahorses use their tails to hang on to seaweed and the males look after the eggs in a special pouch. Some deep-sea fish have branches extending from them and can make a light at the end to lure prey.

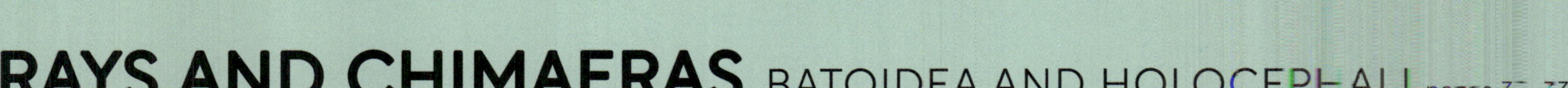

RAYS AND CHIMAERAS BATOIDEA AND HOLOCEPHALI pages 32–33

These are cartilaginous fish which means their skeleton is not made of bone but of cartilage. Cartilage is in your ears and the end of your nose.

Rays have flattened bodies and enlarged fins that look like wings. They seem to fly through water. Electric rays can produce a powerful shock to kill prey or to get themselves out of danger.

Sawfish have a snout that looks like a long blade with teeth on either side.

Some rays have a whiplike tail with a barbed spine on the end. This has a poison gland in it.

Manta rays can be nearly 23-feet wide and can leap right out of the water.

Chimaeras have bulky heads and have just six large teeth that continuously grow.

SHARKS SELACHII pages 34–35

Sharks are cartilaginous fish, like rays. They do not have a swim bladder but they have oily livers that help them with buoyancy or keeping them afloat.

Fossil records show sharks dating back 400 million years, so they have been around for a long time.

Sharks are top predators and are very important in the marine ecosystem. They hunt the animals that graze on sea plants, which keeps their numbers in check and prevents overgrazing. Sea plants are extremely important in the oceans for absorbing carbon dioxide.

Sharks are hunted by humans for their fins and as food so now many species are in danger of extinction. Sharks grow slowly so it takes a long time for them to make up their numbers.

The biggest fish in the world is the whale shark which is approximately 40-feet long. It feeds on tiny plankton by sieving the sea water through special filter pads.

Shark teeth are constantly replaced throughout their lives. Rows of replacement teeth steadily move forward to replace old and worn teeth. A shark can lose 30,000 teeth in its lifetime.

Mermaid purses, often found on beaches, are the dried leathery eggshells of sharks and rays. The eggs hatch inside the mother's body so the young are born alive and fully functional. Some baby sharks eat the unhatched eggs, so it is an advantage to be the first hatched!

WHALES, KILLER WHALES, DOLPHINS, NARWHALS

CETACEANS pages 36–37

These animals are mammals. Mammals are vertebrates and are warm-blooded which means their body temperature remains constant despite the temperature outside. Mammals also grow their babies in their bodies and feed their babies with milk produced by mammary glands. Mammals have hair or fur, although these mammals have hair only before they are born!

The blue whale is the biggest animal ever known to have existed on Earth. It can reach approximately 100 feet in length.

There are two types of cetaceans, toothed whales and baleen whales. Toothed whales include dolphins, porpoises, orcas, sperm whales, and beaked whales. These animals hunt fish, squid, and other marine invertebrates. Orcas hunt seals and have been seen to work together to catch their prey.

Baleen whales include the blue whale, bowhead whale, right whale, and gray whale. They have bristles instead of teeth and filter out small invertebrates from seawater, so the biggest creature in the world, the blue whale, feeds on some of the smallest creatures, krill.

Cetaceans have been hunted for their meat, blubber, and oil for centuries and many species are now threatened with extinction. Climate change has made the situation worse.

SEA LIONS, SEALS, MANATEES

SIRENIANS AND PINNIPEDS pages 38–39

These animals are all mammals. Sea lions and seals are semi-aquatic carnivores, living most of their lives in water. They come out on land to mate and give birth, or to escape predators like sharks and orcas.

Seals and sea lions are perfectly adapted for swimming with their streamlined bodies and fins for limbs. Sea lions and fur seals have obvious ears, whereas other seals do not. Most seals and sea lions eat fish, though the leopard seal hunts penguins and other seals, and the walrus seal feeds on bottom dwelling mollusks.

Dugongs and manatees are fully aquatic and do not come out on to land, but they do come to the surface of the water to breathe. Their babies are born underwater and the mother helps them to the surface to take their first breath.

Dugongs and manatees graze on sea grasses and are sometimes called sea cows. Like many aquatic animals, dugong and manatee populations are suffering from human interference and pollution of the seas.

PRIMATES PRIMATES pages 40–41

Primates are a very diverse group of mammals, including lemurs, lorises, monkeys, and apes, and they are among the most sociable of all animals. Primates have big brains, bigger than any other land-living mammal when compared with their body weight. They have flat nails, not claws or hooves like other mammals, and forward-facing eyes that can see in color. Some primates have an opposable thumb, which helps them grasp branches and hold tools, such as twigs, which they poke into holes to get food.

Primates are very vocal mammals and use facial expressions to convey their feelings. Chimpanzees can distinguish faces of familiar and unfamiliar individuals.

The smallest primate is the Madam Berthe's mouse lemur which weighs approximately 1 ounce. The largest is the gorilla, weighing 300–400 pounds.

WOLVES AND FOXES CANIDAE pages 42–43

Canines are carnivorous mammals. They all have a similar body shape with long noses, upright ears, bushy tails, and teeth for cracking bones and slicing flesh.

Many like to live in sociable groups. Foxes and dogs often live in family groups of a male and female and their young. Both parents look after the youngsters.

Wolves and African wild dogs live in bigger groups, called packs, which hunt larger prey and may be led by one dominant individual.

Canines use urine to mark their territory. They communicate through gestures, growls, barks, and scent signals from their urine.

The domestic dog has been man's best friend for thousands of years and is a descendant of the wolf.

LIONS, TIGERS, LEOPARDS, CATS FELIDAE pages 44–45

Felines are cats. They are carnivorous mammals, too. Most cats are spotty or stripy. They have sharp claws which they can retract into their paws, except for cheetahs. Usually cats are quiet animals, but they may purr when content and snarl and spit when fighting or threatened. Big cats, such as lions, tigers, leopards, and jaguars can roar and growl.

Most cats are good climbers and are at home in trees, though lions, tigers, and cheetahs tend to stay on the ground.

Cats tend to be solitary. They hunt by creeping up on their prey then chasing it. Lions are an exception to this. They are very sociable and live in large groups called prides, sometimes numbering 30. Female lions hunt together, singling out suitable prey then chasing it.

The cheetah is the fastest of mammals, reaching speeds of over 60 miles an hour!

HYENAS, GENETS, MONGOOSES FELIFORMIA pages 46–47

These mammals are catlike and some have retractable claws.

Hyenas are one of Africa's top predators. Their jaws are among the strongest in relation to size of any other mammal. They make a lot of noises and are particularly known for a laughter-like sound. This can be heard up to 3 miles away and is used to tell other clan members that they have found food.

Genets have retractable claws. They are good at climbing trees to hunt birds. They also eat eggs and fruit. Like cats, they prefer to live alone and when frightened they can squirt a nasty smelling substance to put off their attacker.

Mongooses are famous for attacking venomous snakes. They are very fast and agile, darting at the head of the snake and biting its skull. They do get bitten but have something in their blood that breaks down snakes' venom.

Meercats are small mongooses that live in large groups. Some individuals keep a lookout for predators by standing upright and constantly looking around. Everyone dives down a burrow when the alarm call is given.

Unlike other animals in this group, the aardwolf eats insects, mainly termites, which it laps up with its sticky tongue.

HORSES AND ZEBRAS EQUIDAE pages 48–49

Equines, such as horses and zebras, are odd-toed, hoofed mammals that walk on one hoofed toe. Horses are adapted to run from predators. They have long legs and a great sense of balance. They can sleep standing up and lying down. Horses have the biggest eyes of any land mammal and as they are positioned at the sides of their heads, it means they have 340 degrees of almost panoramic vision.

Przewalski's horses is the only truly wild horse left—the others having all been domesticated.

Zebras are African equines with striking black and white stripes. The stripes are different for each animal, like fingerprints.

The donkey is a domesticated ass descended from the African wild ass and has been used as a work animal for about 5,000 years. The noise they make—a loud bray—can be heard nearly 2 miles away.

BULLS, BISONS, BUFFALOES BOVIDAE pages 50–51

Bovines are even-toed, hoofed mammals. Their hooves are split into two toes and they have permanent horns.

Cattle are an important food source for humans. They are kept for their hides, milk, and meat all around the world, except parts of India and Nepal where they are considered sacred. Other bovines have been domesticated, such as the water buffalo and the yak.

Bovines have a four-chambered stomach system to enable them to digest tough plant matter.

The American bison used to live in huge herds on the plains of North America before their numbers were decimated by hunting for their hides and meat.

Yaks are heavily built bovines with long shaggy hair and a dense woolly undercoat to keep them warm.

SHEEP, CHAMOIS, GOATS CAPRINAE pages 52–53

These mammals are even-toed and have a similar digestive system to bovines. They are sociable animals and live in groups called flocks. They graze on grasses and move together following a leader on to fresh pastures.

Sheep and goats were one of the earliest animals to be domesticated. They are kept for their meat, milk, and fleece. Domestic sheep are thought to be descended from the Mouflon that lives in southwest and central Asia.

Wild sheep tend to live in hilly or mountainous areas. They are very good at walking along rocky, narrow ledges. Both the males (rams) and females (ewes) have horns whereas domestic sheep may or may not have horns depending on the breed.

Wild sheep often run to higher ground when threatened but they will also fight back. Goats are naturally curious. They are agile and can climb and balance in precarious places. They can even climb trees! Male goats are called bucks or billies and usually have a beard. Females are called does or nannies, and youngsters are called kids.

The musk ox and takin are the biggest and bulkiest of the sheep and goat family.

WILD BOARS, PIGS, HIPPOPOTAMUSES

SUINA AND HIPPOPOTAMIDAE pages 54–55

Pigs, wild boars, and hippos are even-toed, hoofed mammals.

Domestic pigs are farmed for their meat. Hippos look like pigs but are in fact more closely related to Cetaceans (whales and dolphins) according to more recent research. Although they look bulky, they move gracefully in water and can run fast on land! They use their tails to flick their dung around to mark their territory.

The wild boar is one of the widest ranging mammals in the world. They are very adaptable to different habitats and have become a nuisance in some areas.

Warthog males have two pairs of tusks that are used for fighting in the mating season.

MICE, SQUIRRELS, RABBITS, HARES

RODENTS AND LAGOMORPHS pages 56–57

Rodents are mammals with a single pair of continuously growing incisors (front teeth) in their upper and lower jaws.

Rabbit, hares, and pikas are lagomorphs, not rodents. They have four incisors in the upper jaw that continue to grow throughout their lives. In fact, all their teeth continue growing so they spend a lot of time chewing plants to keep them in check.

About forty percent of all mammal species are rodents. They live all over the world in all sorts of habitats, so they are a very successful group. The largest is the capybara which can weigh 145 pounds, whereas most rodents weigh less than 4 ounces. Porcupines have sharp spines which they use in defense. The chinchilla has extremely soft, silky fur and was nearly wiped out by the fur trade.

Rats and the house mouse have spread all over the world in association with humans and have caused a lot of problems. They can carry disease around the world with their fleas. Rats jumping from ships onto islands can also kill off huge numbers of birds.

HEDGHOGS, MOLES, SHREWS

EULIPOTYPHLA, AFROSORCIDA, AND DERMOPTERA pages 58–59

These mammals tend to have a pointy snout, sharp teeth, and eat insects, worms, and other small invertebrates.

Hedgehogs are spiny mammals that roll into a ball when threatened, tucking in their furry face, feet, and belly. They are mainly nocturnal, meaning active at night. Hedgehogs can be quite noisy with their grunting and sniffing in the hedgerows. They hibernate in winter to survive the cold and lack of food. Hibernation is more than a deep sleep—it means their body temperature drops and their heart rate and metabolism slow down.

Shrews are always busy, so they eat constantly to keep their energy levels. Moles have velvety fur, tiny eyes and ears, and very powerful front limbs adapted for digging. They live underground in a maze of tunnels. They can sense when a worm drops through the soil into their tunnel and they rush to eat it.

Giant otter shrews are great swimmers. They are not shrews or otters, but they look like a shrew and swim like an otter.

Tenrecs are only found on the island of Madagascar. They have a wide variety of form, some are hedgehog-like, some are shrewlike, some live in trees, some in water.

WEASELS, OTTERS, SKUNKS

MUSTELIDAE, MEPHITIDAE, AND PROCYONIDAE pages 60–61

These mammals are long-bodied, short-legged, and they smell. They use the scent glands in their bottoms to mark their territories! They are busy animals, active and inquisitive, and they are carnivores, hunting a wide range of animals. Some are valued for their fur, such as mink.

Most mustelidae live solitary lives, except for the Eurasian badger, sea otters, and some species of river otter. Weasels are aggressive predators and can chase rodents through their burrows as they have narrow bodies that can fit through small places.

Sea otters live on the coast and spend most of their time in the sea. They have fully webbed feet and large lungs for long dives. Sea otters can sleep at sea, often in groups, holding each other's front feet to form rafts, near beds of kelp.

Skunks have striking black-and-white stripes. These markings are a warning signal to other animals not to mess with them. They can produce a really bad smelling liquid and actively squirt it between 3 and 20 feet!

BEARS AND PANDAS

URSIDAE AND AILURIDAE pages 62–63

Bears are mammals. They have large bodies, stocky legs, short tails, and small ears. They have an excellent sense of smell, even better than dogs, and use this sense to help them find food. Despite looking heavy, they can move fast for short distances. Most bears are omnivores, meaning they eat plants and animals, but the giant panda is mostly herbivorous, eating bamboo. The polar bear is mostly carnivorous, hunting seals. Together with the Kodiak bear, polar bears are the largest of bears measuring 8 to 10 feet in length. The smallest bear is the sun bear which is only 3 to 4.5 feet in length.

The brown bear goes fishing when the salmon migrate up rivers to spawn. They can be seen in large groups trying to catch the slippery fish. Young bears (cubs) try to fish, too. They must learn this skill for when they fend for themselves. The fish help the bears put on a layer of fat to help them through cold winters.

Bears rub their backs on trees to leave their scent behind and also remove loose fur and parasites. Polar bears leave their scent in their tracks. This is so individuals can communicate with one another.

DEER, ROE DEER, ELK CERVIDAE pages 64–65

Deer are even-hoofed mammals, walking on two toes. They browse or graze on vegetation and have a ruminant digestion (similar to cows and sheep) to help them digest tough plant material.

Most male deer grow antlers each year and shed them after the mating season. Each year the antlers get bigger, and more points appear. Antlers are used by male deer to signal how fit and strong they are, and to fight other males who try to take over their group of females.

Female reindeer also grow antlers, which is unique among deer. Reindeer are found in the cold north, so they have a heavy, furry coat to keep them warm. They have hooves that can spread on snow to keep their footing and they travel between tundra and forests in huge herds of up to half a million animals.

Water deer do not have antlers. The males have tusks instead.

Red deer stags are known to bellow loudly to challenge other males.

Deer meat is called venison and their hides are known as buckskin.

GAZELLES, WILDEBEEST, ANTELOPES

BOVIDAE pages 66–67

Antelopes are even-hoofed mammals walking on two toes, like deer and with a similar digestion. The difference between deer and antelopes is antelopes do not shed their horns every year as they are made of bone and grow steadily throughout their lives. If they are damaged, they remain broken.

More species of antelope are native to Africa than any other continent. Most live on the grassy plains, known as savannahs, and undertake long migrations following the rains to fresh grazing.

Gazelles and springbok are fast runners and high jumpers to evade predators such as lions and cheetahs. The Thomson's gazelle has been recorded at a maximum speed of 55 miles an hour. Impala can jump 10 feet high.

Antelopes have adapted to other habitats as well. The saiga antelope lives in cold regions and has a swollen snout to warm air as it breathes in. It also has a good sense of smell.

The Arabian oryx is adapted to living in deserts. Its white coat reflects the sun and splayed hoofs help it walk on sand. Gerenuk will stand on its back legs to reach tasty tree foliage.

GIRAFFES, LLAMAS, DROMEDARIES, CAMELS

GIRAFFIDAE AND CAMELIDAE pages 68–69

Camels and llamas have two-toed feet with toenails and soft foot pads. This makes them distinctly different from other hoofed animals. They walk and run by moving both legs on one side together. Riding a camel feels different to riding a horse as they sway from side to side.

Camels are nicknamed "ships of the desert" as they are so well suited to a hot, dry environment. Their humps store fatt for when food is short. Having all this stored fat in one place rather than spread around their body helps keep them cool. The hump sags when the camel has used its store of fat. Camels have been domesticated for many thousands of years and help humans survive in desert climates.

Llamas are social animals and live with others in a herd. Both llamas and alpacas have been domesticated for centuries and alpacas in particular are known for their soft wool.

When llamas and camels are annoyed, they can spit. The spit is regurgitated food from the stomach mixed with saliva and can travel up to 11 yards!

Giraffes are the world's tallest mammals and their tongue can be up to 20 inches long and a blue-ish color.

Each giraffe has a different coat pattern, just as all humans have a different fingerprint.

RHINOCEROSES, ELEPHANTS, TAPIRS, HYRAXES

PROBOSCIDEA, PERRISODACTYLA, AND HYDRACOIDEA pages 70–71

Rhinoceroses (or rhinos) were once found across Europe, Asia, and Africa but now they are only found in national parks in Asia and Africa. They can weigh over half a ton and have very thick skin with one or two horns on their nose. African rhinos lack front teeth so use the front of their mouths to pluck leaves and twigs to eat.

Elephants are the largest living land mammals—the African elephant can weigh up to 18,000 pounds. The trunk is an elongation of the upper lip and nose. It has many uses such as stroking a calf, sucking up water to drink or spray, and using a branch to scratch itself where it cannot reach.

Elephant tusks are big front teeth made of ivory. Unfortunately, this means these animals are hunted by poachers. Elephants live in family groups led by an old, knowledgeable female. They have the longest pregnancy of any mammal—18 to 20 months!

Hyraxes are small, hoofed mammals whose closest relative is the elephant!

Tapirs love to wallow in mud and cool off in rivers. Their babies are spotty and stripy unlike their mom and dad.

ARMADILLLOS AND SLOTHS

XENARTHRA, TUBULIDENTATA, PHOLIDOTA, AND MONOTREMES pages 72–73

Armadillo means “little-armored one.” Their bodies are covered with hard plates called carapace and have bands of hard material across their backs to give flexibility. Sloths are tree dwellers and spend most of their time hanging upside down and sleeping. They move very slowly, eating leaves as they go. Sometimes their fur can look greenish due to algae growing on the long hairs.

Anteaters have very long snouts and a sticky tongue, perfect for licking up ants and termites. The giant anteater’s tongue can be almost 2 feet long. They live in Central and South America.

Aardvarks have long snouts and tongues for eating ants just like anteaters but live in Africa.

Pangolins are the only mammals completely covered in scales. They can roll up into a ball if threatened.

The platypus and echidna are unusual animals because, although they are mammals, they lay eggs! They still feed their babies milk but instead of the young sucking on a teat, the milk just oozes out of glands.

KANGAROOS AND OPOSSUMS MARSUPIALS pages 71–75

These mammals are marsupials. This means their babies start off growing inside the mother but are born very young and crawl into a pouch on the mother's tummy where they latch on to a teat to continue their development.

Kangaroos have very powerful back legs and a long, strong tail. The biggest species can leap 30 feet in a single jump. Their babies are called joeys and stay in the mother's pouch until they are about 10 months old.

Opossums are marsupials found in the Americas. When threatened they pretend to be dead and even smell like a dead animal.

Possums are different to opossums and live in Australia. They are still marsupials but they have a variety of forms. Some can glide between trees such as the sugar glider. Some are monkey-like such as the cuscus.

Koalas mainly live in eucalyptus trees feeding on the leaves. Eucalyptus leaves are not very nutritious, so koalas tend to be slow moving and sleep a lot.

BATS CHIROPTERA pages 76–77

Bats are mammals that can fly, not just glide. They are more agile in flight than most birds.

Flying foxes are the largest bats in the world and have a wingspan up to 6.5 feet. The smallest is the bumblebee bat weighing less than an ounce. It is the smallest mammal in the world.

Some bats use echolocation to hunt night-flying insects. They send out a high frequency sound and listen to the echo to pinpoint their prey. Other bats eat frogs, fruit, nectar, fish, and even blood.

The tube-lipped nectar bat has a tongue more than one and a half times longer than its body to reach nectar at the bottom of long tubular flowers.

Vampire bats make a small cut on an animal then lap up the blood with their tongues. They can sense the sound of an animal breathing and unlike most bats they can walk, run, and jump to help them attach to their prey.

Bats roost upside down. Their weight keeps their joints locked, so they do not have to actively grip all the time.

BIRDS AVES pages 78–87

Birds are warm-blooded vertebrates that have feathers covering their bodies. They are actually feathered dinosaurs, which makes them the only known living dinosaurs! Their closest living relative is the crocodile.

Birds have beaks with no teeth, lay hard-shelled eggs, and have a lightweight, but strong, skeleton. They have a unique digestive system and can store swallowed food. The range of color, pattern, size, and habits is enormous.

Beaks come in a huge variety of shape and size—from the curved sharp beaks of eagles, ideal for tearing prey, to long, curved beaks of the curlew, used for probing food in mud and sand. The flamingo beak sieves the water for tiny animals to eat, and the parrot can crack tough nuts with its strong beak.

The largest bird is the ostrich at a height of 9 feet, and the smallest is the bee hummingbird at 2 inches long.

Some birds, such as the ostrich and kiwi, have lost the ability to fly. Penguins have wings which are adapted to "fly" underwater.

Hummingbirds can beat their wings so fast they "hum" and can fly in any direction like a helicopter.

INDEX

Note: Page numbers in **bold** indicate summaries of group traits/characteristics.